FROM HIS HEART TO YOURS...

AND BACK AGAIN

Scripture-based prayers for Christian writers

Book 1: Ephesians

by NATASHA WOODCRAFT

BROAD PLACE
publishing
broadplacepublishing.co.uk

First published in Great Britain in 2024

Broad Place Publishing

https://broadplacepublishing.co.uk

email: admin@broadplacepublishing.co.uk

Copyright © Natasha Woodcraft 2024

The author has asserted her right under Section 77 of the Copyright, Designs and Patents Act, 1988, to be identified as the author of the work.

All rights reserved. No portion of the book may be reproduced or transmitted in any form or by any means, electronic or mechanical, including photocopying and recording, or by any information storage and retrieval system, without permission in writing from the publisher.

Scripture quotations are taken from the *Holy Bible*, New Living Translation, copyright ©1996, 2004, 2015 by Tyndale House Foundation. Used by permission of Tyndale House Publishers, Carol Stream, Illinois 60188. All rights reserved.

The views and opinions expressed in this work are those of the author and do not necessarily reflect the views and opinions of the publisher.

A catalogue record for this book is available from the British Library.

ISBN: 978-1-915034-86-1

All proceeds from the sale of this book are dedicated to the Kingdom Story Writers

HOW TO USE THIS BOOK

It's my heart's desire and passion to see greater numbers of Christians owning the Scripture as their source – the lamp to their feet – not just in life, but in their creative expression. Creativity is part of our 'imaging' of God. We have a deep-seated need to connect spiritually with the Creator and the creation, expressing ourselves with beauty, wonder, sorrow and joy. This might be through art, music, sculpture, dance etc. but as you're reading this, I assume you express yourself through writing. I believe all creativity can be for the glory of the One who designed it.

Scripture is a work of art. The storytellers, writers, editors and compilers didn't just scribble their thoughts haphazardly, but considered the structure, language and form, right down to individual letter shapes. We often miss these details in our translations, but, I believe if we dwell in the Word, abiding in it, the Holy Spirit reveals to us its greater depths.

This little book is intended to give you time to dwell.

It is intended to give you opportunity to commit your creativity to the Creator.

Rather than pull favourite verses out of context, a full book has been considered, expanded and personalised. In this way, I hope the Word – Jesus – can speak through His word to your heart, and you can speak through His word back to

His heart! There is power in praying Scripture. When we pray Scripture, we can be sure we are praying in the Father's will, and what we ask for will be granted (1 John 5:14-15).

So how should you use this book?

The short answer is – however you like!

The longer answer is – there is a certain design to it.

Each week considers one section of Scripture as a prayer and breaks it down into five parts – one for each weekday. One Bible verse is highlighted each day, but I'd encourage you, if you have time, to read the entire passage, so it can sink deep. You may wish to pray each small part, or build the whole prayer up over the week – it's entirely up to you. I haven't added the 'Amen' until the end of the week! There is journaling space to add your personal thoughts, or anything God speaks to you as you pray.

At the end of each week is a Selah: an opportunity to pause and listen. You may like to make this your Friday devotion, or make time for it at the weekends, but please resist the urge to skip it altogether. It isn't a catch up page; it's a consolidation page.

There are so many names for God in the Scriptures. Interestingly, 'God' isn't really used as a name like we use it, but as a noun. God is what He is, rather than who He is. Jesus tells us when we pray to cry, 'Abba,' (Daddy) and I tend to use this endearment more and more as I get to know my God.

I don't know what your favourite way of addressing God is, but as I wrote these prayers, I felt led to leave most of the introductions blank. Perhaps you can use your favourite 'My...' or perhaps you could try praying with some of the names that Scripture uses. I've listed some below. Maybe think about which name best expresses something from each prayer?

This isn't an exhaustive list. Do add your own in the blank spaces. He is your abba, and He loves to hear your voice!

Names for God:

Father (Abba), Son (Jesus / Yeshua), Holy Spirit (Ruach)
The Trinitarian Creator (Elohim)
The God who Sees (El Roi)
God Almighty (El Shaddai)
The Everlasting God (El Olam)
The Living God (El Chay)
I AM (Yahweh – The Lord's name)
Yahweh, my Provider (Yahweh Yireh / Jehovah Jireh)
The Lord / My Master (Adonai)
Yahweh, my Healer (Yahweh Rophe)
Yahweh, my Banner (Yahweh Nissi)
The Jealous God (El Kanna)
The Holy One (Qedosh)
Yahweh, my Peace (Yahweh Shalom)
The Lord of Hosts (Yahweh Tsebaoth)
The God Most High (El Elyon)
Yahweh, my Rock (Yahweh Tsuri)
Yahweh, my Shepherd (Yahweh Roi)
Yahweh, my Righteousness (Yahweh Tsidqenu)
Yahweh, who is There (Yahweh Shammah)
God with Us (Immanuel)

Descriptions for God, also used as titles:

The Name
The King
The Husband
The Dwelling Place
The Refuge
The Shield
The Fortress
The Strong Tower
The Judge
The Hope of Israel
The Anointed One (Christ / Messiah)
The Comforter
Prince of Peace
Salvation (Yeshua - this is Jesus' literal name!)
Wonderful Counsellor

My favourites & My own:

– WEEK 1 –

Reading: Ephesians 1:1-14

We probably shouldn't have favourite Scriptures, but Paul's astonishing letter to the Ephesians has got to be in my top three, along with Matthew and Isaiah. It is so full of gold that you could mine it for a lifetime and still find something new every day.

Paul lays out God's cosmic purposes in this first section – and the crazy bit? We are blessed in the heavenly realms, chosen before the creation of the world, chosen to be holy, adopted into His family... the list goes on and on.

Though absolutely Christ-centric, this passage from Ephesians is also you-centric. Me-centric. We are invited into God's cosmic story. So, as you write stories for His kingdom and glory, remember that you are part of His story.

It doesn't get more astonishing than that!

PRAYER 1

'Even before he made the world, God loved us and chose us in Christ to be holy and without fault in his eyes.'

Ephesians 1:4

Oh, my Abba, my Lord and my God,

You are so blessed, and so worthy of praise.
May Your father-heart bless me
      with every spiritual blessing in heaven's fountain
      as I dwell in Jesus, my Saviour.
You chose me in Christ,
selected me as Your own before You said,
      'Let there be light.'
You chose me to be holy,
      so, make me different,
set me apart for You.
Oh, purify everything I do
      until it is blameless in Your sight,
Including what I write.

Journaling space

PRAYER 2

'God decided in advance to adopt us into his own family by bringing us to himself through Jesus Christ.'

Ephesians 1:5

My ……………………………………,

I praise You!
For You lovingly planned for me to be
      adopted as Your own child.
It was Your good pleasure to do this –
      to redeem me and to own me.
May all my creativity
      bring honour to Your name,
flow out of abundant gratitude,
      and bless my fellow sisters and brothers.
You adopted me for the praise of Your glorious grace –
      the favour which You so freely clothed me with –
in and through Your beloved Jesus, my Saviour.
I thank You for this indescribable gift.

Journaling space

PRAYER 3

'He is so rich in kindness and grace that he purchased our freedom with the blood of his Son and forgave our sins.'

Ephesians 1:7

My ………………………………………….,

I can never praise You enough!
You are so good!
In Jesus, I have deliverance and salvation
    through His lifeblood which,
        spilt as it was at the cross,
        ran over the altar,
        onto the floor and pooled at my feet.
I kneel in that blood. It washes me clean.
It purifies me,
    providing complete pardon for my sin,
    my rebellion, my wrongdoing.
This is the richness of Your grace
    which You have not just held out tentatively
    but have lavished upon me.
This is how kind You are.
    How much You love me!
I rest in Your grace and ask You to fill me with it,
    that it may flow out from me into my words.

Journaling space

PRAYER 4

'God has now revealed to us his mysterious will regarding Christ—which is to fulfil his own good plan.'

Ephesians 1:9

My ....,

Help me to know Jesus better.
Into deeper communion draw me
       that I may know the mysteries of Your will,
       the wonders You have designed,
       according to Your good pleasure.
I know You will bring all things together in Christ.
I want to be part of that.
So I bring everything – I offer it up –
Everything that touches heaven and earth;
       for my inheritance is Jesus.
       My destiny is with You.
       You have claimed me as Your own.
May I write to make that known.

Journaling space

PRAYER 5

'And when you believed in Christ, he identified you as his own by giving you the Holy Spirit, whom he promised long ago.'

Ephesians 1:13b

My ....,

I once was far off.
    I wasn't interested in You.
    I belonged to the world.
Then I heard the truth –
    The glorious truth of Your saving grace
    The wonderful truth of Your sacrifice
    The amazing truth of Your resurrection power
And I believed.
And you said, 'I'm Yours.'
So seal me, Holy Spirit;
Be my guarantee –
    the foretaste of my promised possession.
Which is You, Glorious One.
    My God.
You are the only possession I want and need.
To my God be the glory,
    in everything I write.

To my God be the glory:
    Inspired by You,
    is all I do.

      Amen

Journaling space

SELAH

At the end of a busy week,

here's your chance to pause.

Be still in God's presence.

Let what you've prayed this week sink into your soul,

and let God speak.

What is He saying to you right now?

– WEEK 2 –

Reading: Ephesians 1:15-23

As we continue in Ephesians, Paul's attention turns to the church. In his beautiful prayer, he prays that the Ephesian believers might have all the things we're going to pray for: A spirit of wisdom and revelation, the eyes of their hearts enlightened... It can feel a bit bold to request all these things, but it's scriptural!

Paul is praying this corporately, for our church family are part of our inheritance. Have you ever thought of that before?

I hope you have prayer support from your church. If you don't, please ask for it. If you don't yet know a group of Kingdom writers – please hunt for one. They are uniquely placed to understand and encourage you.

I sometimes feel that writing in partnership with the Holy Spirit requires a daily infilling. Every time words flow onto my page, I want them to come from Him. As we're giving out, we need to remember to feed on the Lord. That's why reminding ourselves of all the truths about Jesus' majesty in these prayers is so important. He is so awesome!

PRAYER 1

'I pray for you constantly, asking God, the glorious Father of our Lord Jesus Christ, to give you spiritual wisdom and insight so that you might grow in your knowledge of God.'

Ephesians 1:17

Precious Jesus, my Saviour,

Thank You for giving me sisters and brothers
    to join me on my writing journey.
Merciful God,
    Father of my Lord Jesus Christ,
    Grant us deep and intimate insight
    into the true knowledge of Jesus,
        who is *The Way* to You, Abba Father.
Grant to me, and to my fellow siblings:
    Wisdom that exceeds all earthly wisdom,
    and insight that exceeds that of Solomon.
Because we know Jesus,
    whom Solomon could only glimpse forward to.
May I write with even greater wisdom than he,
    For I have access to a greater truth.
    through Your Holy Spirit in me.

Journaling space

PRAYER 2

'I pray that your hearts will be flooded with light so that you can understand the confident hope he has given to those he called—his holy people who are his rich and glorious inheritance.'

Ephesians 1:18

My ....,

May the eyes of my heart –
      the essential centre of my being –
      be enlightened.
Flood me with Your Holy Spirit,
      so I might cherish, with confident expectancy,
the hope You have called me to.
I have a glorious inheritance in my sisters and brothers.
May I treasure the richness of this calling –
      To dwell with them,
      encouraging, admonishing and building up,
Seeing no other writer as a rival
      but spurring each on to godliness
      and Spirit-filled living.
May we write for Your kingdom together,
      Blessing each other.

Journaling space

PRAYER 3

'I also pray that you will understand the incredible greatness of God's power for us who believe him. This is the same mighty power that raised Christ from the dead.'

Ephesians 1:19-20a

My ....,

I believe You have given me Your Holy Spirit,
Therefore, I have immeasurable,
      unlimited, surpassing greatness within me.
The same power that revived Jesus from death
      lives in me!
Help me to believe this,
      to trust Your word,
      to know that You have not given me
      a Spirit of fear
      but of boldness.
It is given to encourage those around me;
      to build Your kingdom here.
Your kingdom looks like this:
      Jesus the Messiah magnified.

Journaling space

PRAYER 4

'Now he is far above any ruler or authority or power or leader or anything else—not only in this world but also in the world to come.'

Ephesians 1:21

My ....,

You raised Jesus from the dead! Then –
Seated Him at Your right hand in the heavenly places,
      far above all rule,
           authority,
                  power and dominion.
No angels or humans can come close –
      He is above all.
Above every name that can ever be named,
      Every title that men may ever claim;
      not only in this age,
      but in the one to come.
So I need not fear.
I need not fear writing truth. For –
No earthly kingdoms,
      or pressures,
           or legislation,
                  can stand against Your purposes.

All these things will pass away
    but You – Jesus Christ – shall remain.
My God, my Lord, my Deliverer.
The Remainer.

Journaling space

PRAYER 5

'And the church is his body; it is made full and complete by Christ, who fills all things everywhere with himself.'

Ephesians 1:23

My ....,

Everything has already been,
    and will always be,
        put under Jesus' feet.
Jesus, You are head over all and especially,
    over Your body, the church.
So, help me to live well with my sisters and brothers,
    who are Your body:
        The temples of Your Spirit on this temporary earth.
Complete in them and in me,
    all Your designed works,
        according to Your wondrous wisdom and power.
May I be Your temple.
Pure, holy and blameless in Your sight.

Amen

Journaling space

SELAH

At the end of another busy week,

here's your chance to pause.

Be still in God's presence.

Let what you've prayed this week sink into your soul,

and let God speak.

What is He saying to you right now?

– Week 3 –

Reading: Ephesians 2:1-10

There's not much about writing in this prayer. Yet I felt convicted that I should include Ephesians 2, although my original intention was to skip to the next of Paul's 'great prayers' in Chapter 3.

I think it's because of this: We are His workmanship (NIV), or as the NLT so beautifully puts it, His masterpiece.

Often as we write Kingdom stories, we'll be writing from our own experiences. This prayer gives you a chance to lay that all before the Lord and claim His grace once again: to remember that you're His workmanship.

It's a huge privilege to write for God's kingdom, but it doesn't win us any 'grace points.' No matter how successful we get (praise Jesus if that's you!) we can boast in Christ alone.

I hope this prayer will protect us from any works-based thinking and keep us humble before His glorious throne of grace.

PRAYER 1

'You used to live in sin, just like the rest of the world, obeying the devil——the commander of the powers in the unseen world. He is the spirit at work in the hearts of those who refuse to obey God.'

Ephesians 2:2

Abba,

Once I was lost.
I was spiritually dead,
    separated from You.
For I had broken Your law:
My inward rebellion was against You.
I walked in that rebellion,
    happy in it, knowing You not.
I followed the ways of this world,
    influenced by its thinking and
    catapulted into darkness.
The words of the deceiver seemed good to me –
    those word's which questioned You
    and shed doubt on Your goodness.
The deceiver still works.
He still battles against my good intentions
    and pervades the world around me.

I see him everywhere:
> In the disobedient.
> In those fighting against Your purposes.
> In those who live by fleshly passions,
> indulging everything they desire.

That was me once.

Now I know better; yet I still struggle.
Without the precious conviction of You, Holy Spirit
> I would be captive again
> to every impulse of my sinful mind;
> under the sentence of Your wrath and
> hopeless, like the rest.

Captivate me, Jesus.
Captivate me so that I shall never be
> captive to him again.

Journaling Space

PRAYER 2

'God is so rich in mercy, and he loved us so much, that even though we were dead because of our sins, he gave us life...'

Ephesians 2:4-5a

God, my God –
>   You are so rich in mercy!
>   You have such great and wonderful love!

You loved me with this: The fullness of Your love.
You chased after me
>   when I was still in darkness.

You broke through and found me and said,
>   'Enough! No more. You are mine.'

Once I was lost.
I was spiritually dead,
>   separated from You,

But You made me spiritually alive.
The same life in the resurrected Jesus
>   You gave to me,
>   defeating death in me.

By Your grace –
>   that unwarranted, unjustifiable merit and favour –
>   You saved me from judgement.

You have raised me up
        and seated me with Jesus
        in the heavenly places.
Thank You.

Journaling Space

PRAYER 3

'For he raised us from the dead along with Christ and seated us with him in the heavenly realms because we are united with Christ Jesus.'

Ephesians 2:6

My ....,

I can barely begin to imagine what this means:
    To be raised with Christ Jesus.
My understanding can but scratch the surface.
As I walk through life,
    it feels so ordinary;
    I don't feel like I am raised with Him.
Yet I know – for You have told me –
    as assuredly as You tell me now,
    that it is done.
    'It is finished.'
    I am raised.
    And it shall be.

So raise me up.
    Raise me up together with Jesus,
    my precious Saviour.

Journaling Space

PRAYER 4

'God saved you by his grace when you believed. And you can't take credit for this; it is a gift from God.'

Ephesians 2:8

My ....,

I am saved by grace!
Show the immeasurable and unsurpassed
    riches of Your grace
        through the work You do *in me*,
        that all might look on me and see Jesus.
Show the immeasurable and unsurpassed
    riches of Your grace
        through all the work I do *for You*,
        that all might look on me and see Jesus.

For it is by unmerited favour You have saved me.
    Not by works.
    I cannot boast.
I want to work for You and with You.
I want to work out my salvation with fear and trembling
    and I pray, 'Help me do this.'
Yet protect me from any notion
    that my work achieves Your love.

As my writing flourishes
— which I believe it will —
protect me from taking undue credit.
For I am Your workmanship.
Your work of art.
Your masterpiece.

Journaling Space

PRAYER 5

'For we are God's masterpiece. He has created us anew in Christ Jesus, so we can do the good things he planned for us long ago.'

Ephesians 2:10

My ....,

I am in awe of that truth:
    That I am Your masterpiece,
    made in Your image.
For I am created anew in Christ Jesus:
    Spiritually transformed by You.
    Renewed for Your good works
    which You prepared in advance for me to do.
I walk into the good life You have made ready.
Whatever I feel like,
    on my good days and my bad days,
    help me remember that You loved me first,
    and Your love never fails.
Nothing I can do will make You love me more
    and nothing I do can make You love me less.
Thank You for chasing after me.
Ignite in me a passion to chase after You.
                        Amen.

Journaling Space

SELAH

At the end of another busy week,

here's your chance to pause.

Be still in God's presence.

Let what you've prayed this week sink into your soul,

and let God speak.

What is He saying to you right now?

– Week 4 –

Reading: Ephesians 2:11-22

Once our lives are changed by the gospel, we naturally want to share that – even though we often live in fear! If you consider yourself a Kingdom writer, I assume you want to share Jesus through your writing.

This prayer puts those desires before our King, asking for the Holy Spirit's help as you partner with Him to illuminate Jesus to the world through your writing. I feel like I need to pray this every day!

It also acknowledges, with Paul, that our personal missions are part of a wider mission: to build up the whole body of Christ into a holy temple. Whether you write primarily for Christians or non-Christians, both can be part of this mission of God's, to not just reconcile the individual to himself, but to build a family of reconciled individuals.

Enjoy cementing your writing into God's amazing plans for the church!

PRAYER 1

'But now you have been united with Christ Jesus. Once you were far away from God, but now you have been brought near to him through the blood of Christ.'

Ephesians 2:12

My God and my Lord,
>Father of all humanity
>and lover of my soul,

Once I was far off.
I was part of the unchosen,
>with no share in the Messianic promise.
I had no hope.
I knew You not.
Then, in the grace of my precious Jesus,
>You brought me near by the blood of my Messiah.
>The blood that unites all believers in You.
Jesus is my peace:
>The bond of unity
>between me and His church.
He smashed every barrier that separated us –
>all walls of spiritual antagonism –
>that nothing should stand.

Journaling Space

PRAYER 2

'For Christ himself has brought peace to us. He united Jews and Gentiles into one people when, in his own body on the cross, he broke down the wall of hostility that separated us.'

Ephesians 2:14

My......................................,

I commit my heart to peace.
As I write, help me prioritise reconciliation
      of the one body
      through Jesus' cross;
      putting to death all resentment.
For Jesus abolished
      all hostility caused by the law
           with its commandments
           and ordinances
           and divisions.
He made us into one people group.
      One humanity.
Help me see all earthly divisions for what they are:
      Abolished.

Journaling Space

PRAYER 3

'He brought this Good News of peace to you Gentiles who were far away from him, and peace to the Jews who were near. Now all of us can come to the Father through the same Holy Spirit because of what Christ has done for us.'
Ephesians 2:17-18

My Jesus,

You preached peace to those far away
        and those who were near.
Through my writing –
        through what You have called me to do –
May I smash barriers,
        showing the way of peace:
Providing for those who are still far off
        to see You,
        to understand,
        and to draw near.
Providing for those who are near
        a new revelation of Your wonder
        through words that You inspire.

It is only through Jesus
        I can directly approach the Father.

Only through Your Holy Spirit
    can I see the truth.
Please reveal any resentment
    that requires my repentance.

Journaling Space

PRAYER 4

'Together, we are his house, built on the foundation of the apostles and the prophets. And the cornerstone is Christ Jesus himself.'

Ephesians 2:20

Holy Spirit,

>In my partnership with other believers,
>especially other Christian writers,
>reveal the Way, the Truth and the Life.

In my creativity:

>May strangers be friends.
>Foreigners belong.
>Outsiders dwell within.

The way is open for all.
Help me live this reality through the way I write.
Help me build on the foundations

>of the apostles and prophets,
>with Jesus as the chief cornerstone
>of all I do.

Keep me firmly situated on His rock.

Journaling Space

PRAYER 5

'We are carefully joined together in him, becoming a holy temple for the Lord.'

Ephesians 2:21

Jesus, my Messiah,

In You, far off people are united.
    May Your Kingdom increase.
May Your church grow into a holy temple –
    A sanctuary dedicated,
    set apart and sacred
    to the presence of God.
In You, Jesus – and in fellowship with Your family –
Make me a dwelling place for God the Holy Spirit.
May this be my motivation.
As I interact with Your church
    in my capacity at a Kingdom writer –
        make me a vessel of Your voice.
As I interact with other writers
    in my capacity as Your precious, beloved child –
        make me a dwelling place of Your Spirit.

Amen

Journaling Space

SELAH

At the end of another busy week,

here's your chance to pause.

Be still in God's presence.

Let what you've prayed this week sink into your soul,

and let God speak.

What is He saying to you right now?

– Week 5 –

Reading: Ephesians 3

Well done. You've made it to Ephesians 3! This is the part you've been waiting for (even if you didn't realise).

The first half of Ephesians 3 is like a summary of all that's gone before, culminating in the declaration that because of Jesus, 'we can now come boldly and confidently into God's presence' (Eph. 3:12b). Wow!

The second half is Paul's incredible prayer of blessing over the Ephesians, where he commits their spiritual growth to the Father, as he falls to his knees in supplication on their behalf.

Paul longs for the Ephesians to be empowered in the Spirit, to know the incredible hugeness of Jesus' love and to be 'made complete with all the fullness of life and power that comes from God' (Eph.3:19b).

Don't you want that for yourself? I certainly do. And the incredible thing is, because Paul prayed this for the Ephesians, and his prayer made it into our Bibles, we know it's absolutely in line with God's will to pray it for ourselves and for others. Yes, it is OK to pray for this incredible experience of God's love and power to be yours. So be bold – pray it!

PRAYER 1

'...God gave me the special responsibility of extending his grace to you Gentiles.'

Ephesians 3:2b

Abba Father,

Like Paul, You have given me a task.
I feel it in my bones:
    I am meant to write for Your glory.
So often I don't feel up to the task.
I know Paul felt that way too:
    insufficient for the task You gave him.
He described himself as the least of the saints.
    Me too!

Yet, You gave him Your unmerited grace
    and commissioned him to preach –
    to proclaim the incomprehensible
    riches of the Messiah.
    To make mysteries plain.
Father, help me proclaim this good news too.
Help me know, and share, the spiritual wealth
    which I don't fully understand,
    but which I know is mine
    in Jesus, my Messiah.

Journaling Space

PRAYER 2

'God's purpose in all this was to use the church to display his wisdom in its rich variety to all the unseen rulers and authorities in the heavenly places.'

Ephesians 3:10

My…………………………………………..,

Help me magnify You,
    the God who created all things and all people.
Help me demonstrate the glorious,
    multifaceted
        wisdom of God
            through what I write.
Our society so often thinks negatively of Your people,
    and of You.
May what I write counter that –
    showing Your beauty,
    holiness and goodness.
May I walk according to Your eternal purposes.
You carried out Your will
    through Jesus' incredible sacrifice.
    Once and for all.
Now, may I follow His example,
    Doing as He did.
    Not my will, but Yours be done.

Journaling Space

PRAYER 3

'Because of Christ and our faith in him, we can now come boldly and confidently into God's presence.'
Ephesians 3:12

My………………………………..,

Give me boldness to approach Your throne of grace
    freely and courageously,
    through faith in Jesus.
For this reason, I kneel before You.
I bow my knees, Abba.
Without You, nothing would exist.
    Not me,
    Nor my reader,
    Nor my page.
You know all the hairs on every head.
Strengthen me from the riches of Your glory,
Energise me with Your power through the Holy Spirit.
Holy Spirit, reach into my inner self,
    all my being and personality,
    and plant Yourself there.

Journaling Space

PRAYER 4

'Then Christ will make his home in your hearts as you trust in him. Your roots will grow down into God's love and keep you strong.'

Ephesians 3:17

Jesus, may You dwell in my heart
    so tangibly that I know You are there
    every minute and every hour.
    Make your home in me.
Root me in Your love.
    Ground me like the deep, deep roots
    of the tallest tree –
    like a Cedar of Lebanon,
    or a Californian Redwood.
Help me comprehend,
    with all God's people:
    the highest heights,
    the deepest depths,
    the longest lengths
    and the widest widths
    of Your unconditional agapé love.
If any doubt exists in my heart,
    telling me You don't love me,
    cast it to the wind.

Counter it with a full experience of
> Your amazing,
> endless adoration –
> the love of the prodigal God
> who ran after me,
> threw His robe around me,
> throwing out all I had done against Him.

May I come to know through personal experience –
> not just information –
> the love of Jesus, my Messiah,
> which far surpasses mere knowledge.

Journaling Space

PRAYER 5

'Then you will be made complete with all the fullness of life and power that comes from God.'

Ephesians 3:19b

My......................................,

Fill me with all the fullness of God,
    the richest experience of Your presence in my life,
    flooding my self with Yourself,
Oh God,
    Creator of the heavens and the earth,
    who stooped to redeem a tiny, beloved one –
    Me!
You are able to carry out Your purposes.
You are able to do superabundantly more
    than all I could dare ask
    or even think:
Infinitely more than my greatest prayers,
    Extravagantly more than my hopes,
    Lavishly more than my dreams.
You can do this according to Your power
    at work in me.
To You – Heavenly Father,
    Magnificent Creator,
    Perfect Redeemer, Lover of my soul –

To You be the glory in me,
>   in Your church,
>   and in Jesus, my Messiah,
>   throughout all generations,
>   forever and ever.

Amen

Journaling Space

SELAH

At the end of another busy week,

here's your chance to pause.

Be still in God's presence.

Let what you've prayed this week sink into your soul,

and let God speak.

What is He saying to you right now?

– Week 6 –

Reading: Ephesians 4

You'll have gathered by now that we are not alone. God never calls us to do something then leaves us to it. Ephesians 4 explores this idea more, so we're going to pray it through in our context as writers.

Our calling is a twofold partnership – with God and with other Christians. Your primary partner in the gospel is the Holy Spirit, and these prayers will invite Him to renew and equip you.

Your secondary partners are other Christians. These might be faithful prayer warriors who've always got your back, praying into breakthrough. This might be other writers who act as critique partners, endorsers or supporters. Praise God for them! There will be space to do that within these prayers. It might also be your church leaders, so we'll consider that too, as Paul does in his letter.

When the whole body of Christ is working together, with Jesus Himself, that's when we see the greatest blessing and the greatest growth. Praying for that is a great privilege and touches the Father's heart.

PRAYER 1

'Therefore I, a prisoner for serving the Lord, beg you to lead a life worthy of your calling, for you have been called by God... Make every effort to keep yourselves united in the Spirit, binding yourselves together with peace.'

Ephesians 4:1-3

My..,

I pray I may live a life worthy of my calling.
Help me exhibit godly character,
      moral courage
      and personal integrity.
May my life radiate gratitude to You
      for my salvation,
      my calling
      and my partners in the gospel.
May I approach the writing You've inspired
      with humility,
      gentleness
      and patience,
      leaning into Your timing in all things
      and leaning on Your word.

Thank You for Your body, the church.
Thank You for unity I've experienced in the Spirit.
Bind us together with peace.
Please provide prayer support for my writing,
    so that many are lifting me up
    as I seek to do Your will,
    and keeping me accountable.

Thank You for those You've already given me
    to support my journey.
Bless the sisters and brothers who pray for me.
I remember them now
    before Your throne of grace.

My supporters are...

PRAYER 2

'However, he has given each one of us a special gift through the generosity of Christ.'

Ephesians 4:7

Abba Father,

Thank You for the gifts You have given me.
Please provide me with fellow godly writers
    who will help me improve my work.
I want it to be the best it can be
    for Your glory.
Give us grace in proportion
    to Christ's rich and abundant gifts.
For when He ascended on high,
    He held captivity captive,
    and He bestowed Your Spirit upon us.
You gave us this gift for writing.
    Give me the grace to bear it and
    put it to good use;
    not storing it up –
    as a man who buries his talents in a field –
    but investing in the Kingdom of God.

Bless my critique partners.

May they approach my writing
> with the same humility and godliness I desire,
> considering it prayerfully.

Thank You for their wisdom.
Keep us united in Your Spirit
Bind us in the bond of peace,
> especially when we must say tough things
> as we critique each other's work.

Help me to be knowledgeable and helpful
> but also kind.

Give me the words to say difficult things in a gentle way.

Journaling Space

PRAYER 3

'Now these are the gifts Christ gave to the church: the apostles, the prophets, the evangelists, and the pastors and teachers. Their responsibility is to equip God's people to do his work and build up the church, the body of Christ.'

Ephesians 4:11-12

Jesus, my Messiah,

In Your church,
You have appointed some to be apostles,
    some prophets, some evangelists,
    some to guide and instruct.
For this purpose:
    To fully equip Your family – which includes me –
    for works of service,
    building up the body of Christ
    until we reach oneness
    in the faith and knowledge
    of the Son of God.
I can't wait for that day of glory!

Abba, bless me with good leaders
    and help me sit well under them,
    learning from them and encouraging them.

May they be part of Your plan to equip me
    for the writing You have called me to.

Where I am a leader,
    fill me with Your Spirit,
        providing all I need to lead well,
        in humility and gentleness,
        as I spur others on to godliness and maturity.

Journaling Space

PRAYER 4

'Then we will no longer be immature like children. We won't be tossed and blown about by every wind of new teaching...'

Ephesians 4:14

My ....,

I ask You for discernment,
       so I may not be like an immature child,
       or a ship on a stormy sea,
       tossed back and forth on the wind.
Instead, be my anchor,
       helping me resist all shifting doctrine,
       deceitfulness and the devil's schemes.
May none of these things ever make their way into my writing, but keep it pure,
       sound
       and abundant with truth.
Regarding truth:
       May I always write truth in love,
       following the example of Jesus, my Messiah.
May my part of Your body work well,
       assisting the whole to grow and mature,
       as You build it up in unselfish agapé love.

Journaling Space

PRAYER 5

'...let the Spirit renew your thoughts and attitudes. Put on your new nature, created to be like God—truly righteous and holy.'

Ephesians 4:23-24

My ....,

I put off my old self,
    completely discarding my former nature.
Instead, continually renew me
    by Your Holy Spirit speaking to my spirit.
Give me a fresh spiritual attitude and
    a new self
    created in Your image –
    blessed with righteous relationships,
    holiness
    and truth.
I reject all falsehood,
I dwell not on anger,
I give the devil no opportunity to lead me into sin
    by continually repenting
    and refusing to cultivate bitterness.
Cleanse my heart so my words are wholesome:
    Good for building others up,
    Full of kindness and compassion,

And a blessing to those who read them.
Let me not grieve the Holy Spirit
    but seal me,
        and mark me for the day of redemption.

Amen

Journaling Space

SELAH

At the end of another busy week,

here's your chance to pause.

Be still in God's presence.

Let what you've prayed this week sink into your soul,

and let God speak.

What is He saying to you right now?

– Week 7 –

Reading: Ephesians 5 & 6

Ephesians 5, and the first part of 6, expand on the difference between walking in the old way and the new way, particularly as regards our relationships with others. We'll consider it briefly but not for too long, as it's not very specific to our writing journey.

The armour of God is where I'd like us to dwell. We need this full armour for every aspect of our lives, but particularly when we're creating and releasing work that glorifies Jesus' name. The devil does not want that work to succeed, and we will often find ourselves in spiritual battles.

This is how we fight our battles – with prayer! The battle can be subtle – discouragement is one of the enemy's most powerful weapons – but it can also be fierce. When you feel like you're surrounded, come back to this week and fight that battle, knowing that after the battle you will still be standing firm. Take courage!

PRAYER 1

'Live a life filled with love, following the example of Christ. He loved us and offered himself as a sacrifice for us, a pleasing aroma to God.'

Ephesians 5:2

My..,

I want to live a life pleasing to You,
      filled with love,
      imitating Your example.
You gave Yourself for me and so now,
      I give myself for You.
Sin has no place among Your people,
      so cast it out of my life.
I was once full of darkness,
      but now I have light from the Lord;
      light which produces goodness and truth.
I awake into my new life.
I rise from the dead
      for Christ to shine in me.
Fill me with Your Spirit –
      with psalms, hymns and spiritual songs
      as I make music in my heart to You.

Help me live in right relationship with
>   those dearest to me
>   and those far away;
>   those in authority over me,
>   and those under my authority.
May I treat all as You would treat them.
For You are my Master in heaven,
>   and You have no favourites.

Journaling Space

PRAYER 2

'A final word: Be strong in the Lord and in his mighty power.'

Ephesians 6:10

To the only God my Saviour,
    Rich in mercy and abundant in faithfulness,

I long to be strong in You.
Draw me to Yourself,
    empowering me through our union,
    in the authority of Your boundless might.
I put on the full armour of God
    that I may successfully stand
    against all the strategies and schemes of the devil,
    who seeks to steal my faith
    and prevent me from fulfilling my calling.
I know this is a spiritual battle.
    He will attack
    when I'm releasing something that honours You
    and builds Your kingdom.
He doesn't want my writing to reach the world.

Therefore, I put on Your full armour,
> that I may successfully stand:
> Fully prepared,
> Immovable
> And victorious.

Journaling Space

PRAYER 3

'Stand your ground, putting on the belt of truth and the body armor of God's righteousness...'

Ephesians 6:14

My ....,

I put on Your full armour:
I tighten the wide band of truth around my waist
    leaning on the promises You've given me.
I put on the breastplate of righteousness
    won for me by Jesus
    who was without sin.
I strap to my feet the gospel of peace,
    knowing this is my message and my salvation.
I lift up the protective shield of faith
    which You've gifted me with
    and built up within me.
    With it, I can extinguish every flaming arrow.
I take the helmet of salvation,
    pushing it firmly on my head,
    where it guards my mind
    from all the devil's lies,
    all his accusations,
    all his claims that I am not good enough.

These lies shall not take my mind captive,
>   for I know whom I have believed.
>   It is not by my works
>   but by the blood of Christ that I am saved.

Journaling Space

PRAYER 4

'Pray in the Spirit at all times and on every occasion. Stay alert and be persistent in your prayers for all believers everywhere.'

Ephesians 6:18

My ....,

Thank You for the Sword of the Spirit
    which I take up now.
That double edged sword
    pierces the hardest hearts.
This sword is Your word,
    illuminated to the softened heart,
    penetrating soul and psyche.
May my words be a sword too,
    sharpened for those
    You have chosen to read them.
Oh, Holy Spirit, prepare hearts to receive Your truth by my pen.

So, I pray.
I pray at all times,
    in every season.
I pray in the Spirit.

Keep me alert,
      watchful,
      prayerful.
      In tune with Your voice.
Keep my armour strong and effective.

Journaling Space

PRAYER 5

'And pray for me, too. Ask God to give me the right words so I can boldly explain God's mysterious plan that the Good News is for Jews and Gentiles alike.'

Ephesians 6:19

My……………………………..,

For others whom You have called to write
    for Your kingdom:
I pray that words may be given to them,
    that when they open their mouths,
    their notebooks or their screens,
    words may flow,
    proclaiming boldly the mystery of good news.
Give us all courage and boldness.
May we be for each other as Tychicus was for the Ephesians:
    A comfort,
    Encouragement
    And strengthener of hearts.
May peace and grace abide
    in all who love my Lord Jesus
    with an undying and incorruptible love. *Amen.*

Journaling Space

SELAH

At the end of this prayer book,

here's your chance to pause.

Be still in God's presence.

Let what you've prayed this week sink into your soul,

and let God speak.

What is He saying to you right now?

FINALLY,

'Peace be with you, dear brothers and sisters, and may God the Father and the Lord Jesus Christ give you love with faithfulness. May God's grace be eternally upon all who love our Lord Jesus Christ.'

Ephesians 6:23-24

ABOUT THE AUTHOR

Natasha Woodcraft lives in a slightly crumbling farmhouse in Lincolnshire with her husband, four sons and a menagerie of animals.

Her published novels, *The Wanderer Scorned* & *The Wanderer Reborn*, explore God's redemptive purposes for messy people by reimagining the tale of Cain & Abel. Also a songwriter, Natasha peppers her emotional prose with poetry and song.

She's part of the team at Broad Place Publishing, a UK publishing house specialising in Christian fiction, and is a member of the Kingdom Story Writers.

ALSO BY THE AUTHOR

The Wanderer Series

"You shall be a fugitive and a wanderer on the earth."

1. The Wanderer Scorned
Cain & Abel reimagined

2. The Wanderer Reborn
Can hope triumph after the first murder?

2.1. The Wanderer's Sister
A Novelette exclusive to the author's newsletter subscribers. Sign up at:
Https://natashawoodcraft.com/subscribe

ABOUT THE PUBLISHER

BROAD PLACE
publishing

Broad Place Publishing is an independent publisher, passionate about bringing to market quality books that Jesus wants the world to read. We look for creative ways to support our authors and distribute our books as widely as possible.

https://broadplacepublishing.co.uk

ABOUT KINGDOM STORY WRITERS

Kingdom Story Writers

Kingdom Story Writers are a UK based team of writers who are passionate about the power of stories, both fiction and non fiction, to carry the truth of the Kingdom.

Our heart is to write God honouring, Holy Spirit inspired, faith building books, that will impact the world we live in – and to see those books published!

https://kingdomstorywriters.co.uk